The Ultimate Mediterranean Cookbook

Easy and Flavorful Meals for Your

Everyday Healthy Diet

Julia Sarkis

Table of Contents

Introduction

Eating a Mediterranean diet can help you to lose weight, lower your risk of heart disease, prevent diabetes and cancer, and support brain health. The Mediterranean diet has been around for more than 3500 years. The first written record of it was by Hippocrates in 400 BC, who wrote about the connection between good health and a balanced diet.

The Mediterranean Diet is one of the most popular diets in the world today. It's a diet that's rich in healthy fats, protein, and whole grains and helps to reduce the risk of cardiovascular disease, diabetes, and obesity. I'm not a nutritionist, but I can tell you that the Mediterranean diet is great for your health because it includes a lot of fruit, vegetables, whole grains, nuts, and olive oils. A lot of people believe the Mediterranean diet is a new diet trend, but it's actually been around for thousands of years.

The Ultimate Mediterranean Cookbook is the ultimate guide to the Mediterranean diet and how you can live a long, healthy life. The Mediterranean diet is renowned for its emphasis on fruits and vegetables, nuts, beans, whole grains and fish. The Mediterranean Diet is a diet that originated in ancient times in Greece and Italy, and it's proven to be extremely healthy for both men and women. The Mediterranean Sea was home to some of the earliest civilizations, and it is one of the most fertile regions in the world. This land is also home to numerous diverse plants and animals, which means that there are so many ways for people to eat.

The Ultimate Mediterranean Cookbook is a collection of recipes from the Mediterranean region, which have been carefully selected by world-renowned chef Mario Batali. The book is a great way to learn about different flavors and ingredients from around the world. The Mediterranean diet is full of good fats and plenty of healthy foods like fruits, vegetables, whole grains, nuts and seeds. It has been linked to a reduced risk of heart disease, diabetes type 2 and stroke. The Mediterranean diet is important for everyone but it's particularly vital to those who are looking to improve their health. When you follow the Mediterranean diet, your body starts to become more resilient and less prone to disease.

"The Ultimate Mediterranean Cookbook" is the first cookbook in my new book series that I'm calling The Mediterranean Kitchen. The Mediterranean diet is all about eating in moderation. This means eating healthy foods like vegetables, fruit, whole grains, nuts and fish. It also means dieting is less of a priority for the Mediterranean diet than it is for a typical American diet. In the Mediterranean, people have been operating in a similar way for thousands of years. Their philosophy is based on living life to the fullest and taking care of others.

The Ultimate Mediterranean Cookbook is a cookbook for foodies and cooks that are interested in the Mediterranean diet. The book begins with a general introduction to what the Mediterranean diet is and how it has been beneficial to humans through history. The Mediterranean Diet is one of the healthiest diets in existence. It's based on a healthy balance of protein, carbs, and calories, while not over-indulging in carbohydrates like bread and pasta. The Mediterranean region is the birthplace of Western civilization. Rome, Greece, and Carthage were all born here and it was a place where all the great empires of the ancient world began to rise.

Breakfast

Hearty Pear and Mango Smoothie

Preparation Time: 10 minutes

Cooking Time: 0 minutes

Servings: 1

Ingredients:

- 1 ripe mango, cored and chopped
- ½ mango, peeled, pitted and chopped
- 1 cup kale, chopped

- ½ cup plain Greek yogurt
- 2 ice cubes

Directions:

1. Add pear, mango, yogurt, kale, and mango to a blender and puree.
2. Add ice and blend until you have a smooth texture.
3. Serve and enjoy!

Lovely Eggplant Salad

Preparation Time: 20 minutes

Cooking Time: 15 minutes

Servings: 8

Ingredients:

- 1 large eggplant, washed and cubed
- 1 tomato, seeded and chopped
- 1 small onion, diced
- 2 tablespoons parsley, chopped
- 2 tablespoons extra virgin olive oil
- 2 tablespoons distilled white vinegar

- ½ cup feta cheese, crumbled
- Salt as needed

Directions:

1. Pre-heat your outdoor grill to medium-high.
2. Pierce the eggplant a few times using a knife/fork.
3. Cook the eggplants on your grill for about 15 minutes until they are charred.
4. Keep it on the side and allow them to cool.
5. Remove the skin from the eggplant and dice the pulp.
6. Transfer the pulp to a mixing bowl and add parsley, onion, tomato, olive oil, feta cheese and vinegar.
7. Mix well and chill for 1 hour.
8. Season with salt and enjoy!

Lovely Artichoke Frittata

Preparation Time: 5 minutes

Cooking Time: 10 minutes

Servings: 4

Ingredients:

- 8 large eggs
- ¼ cup Asiago cheese, grated
- 1 tablespoon fresh basil, chopped
- 1 teaspoon fresh oregano, chopped
- Pinch of salt
- 1 teaspoon extra virgin olive oil

- 1 teaspoon garlic, minced
- 1 cup canned artichokes, drained
- 1 tomato, chopped

Directions:

1. Pre-heat your oven to broil.
2. Take a medium bowl and whisk in eggs, Asiago cheese, oregano, basil, sea salt and pepper.
3. Blend in a bowl.
4. Place a large ovenproof skillet over medium-high heat and add olive oil.
5. Add garlic and sauté for 1 minute.
6. Remove skillet from heat and pour in egg mix.
7. Return skillet to heat and sprinkle artichoke hearts and tomato over eggs.
8. Cook frittata without stirring for 8 minutes.
9. Place skillet under the broiler for 1 minute until the top is lightly browned.
10. Cut frittata into 4 pieces and serve.
11. Enjoy!

Full Eggs in a Squash

Preparation Time: 10 minutes

Cooking Time: 20 minutes

Servings: 5

Ingredients:

- 2 acorn squash
- 6 whole eggs
- 2 tablespoons extra virgin olive oil
- Salt and pepper as needed
- 5-6 pitted dates
- 8 walnut halves
- A fresh bunch of parsley

Directions:

1.   Pre-heat your oven to 375 degrees Fahrenheit.

2.   Slice squash crosswise and prepare 3 slices with holes.

3.   While slicing the squash, make sure that each slice has a measurement of ¾ inch thickness.

4.   Remove the seeds from the slices.

5.   Take a baking sheet and line it with parchment paper.

6.   Transfer the slices to your baking sheet and season them with salt and pepper.

7.   Bake in your oven for 20 minutes.

8.   Chop the walnuts and dates on your cutting board.

9.   Take the baking dish out of the oven and drizzle slices with olive oil.

10.   Crack an egg into each of the holes in the slices and season with pepper and salt.

11.   Sprinkle the chopped walnuts on top.

12.   Bake for 10 minutes more.

13.   Garnish with parsley and add maple syrup.

14.   Enjoy!

The Great Barley Porridge

Preparation Time: 5 minutes

Cooking Time: 25 minutes

Servings: 4

Ingredients:

- 1 cup barley
- 1 cup wheat berries
- 2 cups unsweetened almond milk
- 2 cups water
- ½ cup blueberries
- ½ cup pomegranate seeds
- ½ cup hazelnuts, toasted and chopped
- ¼ cup honey

Directions:

1. Take a medium saucepan and place it over medium-high heat.
2. Place barley, almond milk, wheat berries, water and bring to a boil.
3. Reduce the heat to low and simmer for 25 minutes.
4. Divide amongst serving bowls and top each serving with 2 tablespoons blueberries, 2 tablespoons pomegranate seeds, 2 tablespoons hazelnuts, 1 tablespoon honey.
5. Serve and enjoy!

Cool Tomato and Dill Frittata

Preparation Time: 5 minutes

Cooking Time: 10 minutes

Servings: 4

Ingredients:

- 2 tablespoons olive oil
- 1 medium onion, chopped
- 1 teaspoon garlic, minced
- 2 medium tomatoes, chopped
- 6 large eggs

- ½ cup half and half
- ½ cup feta cheese, crumbled
- ¼ cup dill weed
- Salt as needed
- Ground black pepper as needed

Directions:

1. Pre-heat your oven to a temperature of 400 degrees Fahrenheit.
2. Take a large sized ovenproof pan and heat up your olive oil over medium-high heat.
3. Toss in the onion, garlic, tomatoes and stir fry them for 4 minutes.
4. While they are being cooked, take a bowl and beat together your eggs, half and half cream and season the mix with some pepper and salt.
5. Pour the mixture into the pan with your vegetables and top it with crumbled feta cheese and dill weed.
6. Cover it with the lid and let it cook for 3 minutes.
7. Place the pan inside your oven and let it bake for 10 minutes. Serve hot.

Hearty Strawberry and Rhubarb Smoothie

Preparation Time: 5 minutes

Cooking Time: 3 minutes

Servings: 1

Ingredients:

- 1 rhubarb stalk, chopped
- 1 cup fresh strawberries, sliced
- ½ cup plain Greek strawberries
- Pinch of ground cinnamon
- 3 ice cubes

Directions:

1. Take a small saucepan and fill with water over high heat.
2. Bring to boil and add rhubarb, boil for 3 minutes.
3. Drain and transfer to blender.
4. Add strawberries, honey, yogurt, and cinnamon and pulse mixture until smooth.
5. Add ice cubes and blend until thick with no lumps.
6. Pour into glass and enjoy chilled.

Colorful Bacon and Brie Omelette Wedges

Preparation Time: 10 minutes

Cooking Time: 10 minutes

Servings: 6

Ingredients:

- 2 tablespoons olive oil
- 7 ounces smoked bacon
- 6 beaten eggs
- Small bunch chives, snipped
- 3 ½ ounces brie, sliced
- 1 teaspoon red wine vinegar
- 1 teaspoon Dijon mustard

- 1 cucumber, halved, deseeded and sliced diagonally
- 7 ounces radish, quartered

Directions:

1. Turn your grill on and set it to high.
2. Take a small-sized pan and add 1 teaspoon of oil, allow the oil to heat up.
3. Add lardons and fry until crisp.
4. Drain the lardon on kitchen paper.
5. Take another non-sticky cast iron frying pan and place it over grill, heat 2 teaspoons of oil.
6. Add lardons, eggs, chives, ground pepper to the frying pan.
7. Cook on LOW until they are semi-set.
8. Carefully lay brie on top and grill until the Brie sets and is a golden texture.
9. Remove it from the pan and cut up into wedges.
10. Take a small bowl and create dressing by mixing olive oil, mustard, vinegar and seasoning.
11. Add cucumber to the bowl and mix, serve alongside the Omelette wedges.Enjoy!

Pearl Couscous Salad

Preparation Time: 15 minutes

Cooking Time: 0 minutes

Servings: 6

Ingredients:

For Lemon Dill Vinaigrette

- Juice of 1 large sized lemon
- 1/3 cup of extra virgin olive oil
- 1 teaspoon of dill weed
- 1 teaspoon of garlic powder
- Salt as needed
- Pepper

For Israeli Couscous

- 2 cups of Pearl Couscous
- Extra virgin olive oil
- 2 cups of halved grape tomatoes
- Water as needed
- 1/3 cup of finely chopped red onions
- ½ of a finely chopped English cucumber
- 15 ounces of chickpeas
- 14 ounce can of artichoke hearts (roughly chopped up)
- ½ cup of pitted Kalamata olives
- 15-20 pieces of fresh basil leaves, roughly torn and chopped up
- 3 ounces of fresh baby mozzarella

Directions:

1. Prepare the vinaigrette by taking a bowl and add the ingredients listed under vinaigrette.
2. Mix them well and keep aside.
3. Take a medium-sized heavy pot and place it over medium heat.
4. Add 2 tablespoons of olive oil and allow it to heat up.

5. Add couscous and keep cooking until golden brown.

6. Add 3 cups of boiling water and cook the couscous according to the package instructions.

7. Once done, drain in a colander and keep aside.

8. Take another large-sized mixing bowl and add the remaining ingredients except the cheese and basil.

9. Add the cooked couscous and basil to the mix and mix everything well.

10. Give the vinaigrette a nice stir and whisk it into the couscous salad.

11. Mix well.

12. Adjust the seasoning as required.

13. Add mozzarella cheese.

14. Garnish with some basil. Enjoy!

Simple Coconut Porridge

Preparation Time: 15 minutes

Cooking Time: 0 min

Servings: 6

Ingredients:

- Powdered erythritol as needed
- 1 ½ cups almond milk, unsweetened
- 2 tablespoons va0 minutesla protein powder
- 3 tablespoons Golden Flaxseed meal
- 2 tablespoons coconut flour

Directions:

1. Take a bowl and mix in flaxseed meal, protein powder, coconut flour and mix well.
2. Add mix to saucepan (placed over medium heat).
3. Add almond milk and stir, let the mixture thicken.
4. Add your desired amount of sweetener and serve. Enjoy!

Lunch

Mediterranean Pork Roast

Preparation Time: 10 minutes

Cooking Time: 8 hours and 10 minutes

Servings: 6

Ingredients:

- 2 tablespoons Olive oil
- 2 pounds Pork roast
- ½ teaspoon Paprika
- ¾ cup Chicken broth
- 2 teaspoons dried sage
- ½ tablespoon Garlic minced
- ¼ teaspoon Dried marjoram
- ¼ teaspoon Dried Rosemary
- 1 teaspoon Oregano
- ¼ teaspoon Dried thyme
- 1 teaspoon Basil
- ¼ teaspoon kosher salt

Directions:

1. In a small bowl mix broth, oil, salt, and spices. In a skillet pour olive oil and bring to medium-high heat. Put the pork into it and roast until all sides become brown.

2. Take out the pork after cooking and poke the roast all over with a knife. Place the poked pork roast into a 6-quart crock pot. Now, pour the small bowl mixture liquid all over the roast.

3. Close the crock pot and cook on low heat setting for 8 hours. After cooking, remove it from the crock pot on to a cutting board and shred into pieces. Afterward, add the shredded pork back into the crockpot. Simmer it another 10 minutes. Serve along with feta cheese, pita bread, and tomatoes.

Beef Pizza

Preparation Time: 20 minutes

Cooking Time: 50 minutes

Servings: 10

Ingredients:

For Crust:

- 3 cups all-purpose flour
- 1 tablespoon sugar
- 2¼ teaspoons active dry yeast
- 1 teaspoon salt
- 2 tablespoons olive oil
- 1 cup warm water

For Topping:

- 1-pound ground beef
- 1 medium onion, chopped
- 2 tablespoons tomato paste
- 1 tablespoon ground cumin
- Salt and ground black pepper, as required

- ¼ cup water
- 1 cup fresh spinach, chopped
- 8 ounces artichoke hearts, quartered
- 4 ounces fresh mushrooms, sliced
- 2 tomatoes, chopped
- 4 ounces feta cheese, crumbled

Directions:

For crust:

1. In the bowl of a stand mixer, fitted with the dough hook, add the flour, sugar, yeast and salt. Add 2 tablespoons of the oil and warm water and knead until a smooth and elastic dough is formed.
2. Make a ball of the dough and set aside for about 15 minutes.
3. Place the dough onto a lightly floured surface and roll into a circle. Place the dough into a lightly, greased round pizza pan and gently, press to fit. Set aside for about 10-15 minutes. Coat the crust with some oil. Preheat the oven to 400 degrees F.

For topping:

4. Heat a nonstick skillet over medium-high heat and cook the beef for about 4-5 minutes. Add the onion and cook for about 5 minutes, stirring frequently. Add the tomato paste, cumin, salt, black pepper and water and stir to combine.

5. Reduce the heat to medium and cook for about 5-10 minutes. Remove from the heat and set aside. Place the beef mixture over the pizza crust and top with the spinach, followed by the artichokes, mushrooms, tomatoes, and Feta cheese.

6. Bake for about 25-30 minutes or until the cheese is melted. Remove from the oven and set aside for about 3-5 minutes before slicing. Cut into desired sized slices and serve.

Beef & Bulgur Meatballs

Preparation Time: 20 minutes

Cooking Time: 28 minutes

Servings: 6

Ingredients:

- ¾ cup uncooked bulgur
- 1-pound ground beef
- ¼ cup shallots, minced
- ¼ cup fresh parsley, minced
- ½ teaspoon ground allspice
- ½ teaspoon ground cumin
- ½ teaspoon ground cinnamon
- ¼ teaspoon red pepper flakes, crushed
- Salt, as required
- 1 tablespoon olive oil

Directions:

1. In a large bowl of the cold water, soak the bulgur for about 30 minutes. Drain the bulgur well and then, squeeze with your hands to remove the excess water. In a food processor, add the bulgur, beef, shallot, parsley, spices and salt and pulse until a smooth mixture is formed.

2. Transfer the mixture into a bowl and refrigerate, covered for about 30 minutes. Remove from the refrigerator and make equal sized balls from the beef mixture. In a large nonstick skillet, heat the oil over medium-high heat and cook the meatballs in 2 batches for about 13-14 minutes, flipping frequently. Serve warm.

Tasty Beef and Broccoli

Preparation Time: 10 minutes

Cooking Time: 15 minutes

Servings: 4

Ingredients:

- 1 and ½ pounds flanks steak, cut into thin strips
- 1 tablespoon olive oil
- 1 tablespoon tamari sauce
- 1 cup beef stock
- 1-pound broccoli, florets separated

Directions:

1. In a bowl, mix steak strips with oil and tamari, toss and leave aside for 10 minutes. Set your instant pot on sauté mode, add beef strips and brown them for 4 minutes on each side. Add stock, stir, cover pot again and cook on high for 8 minutes.

2. Add broccoli, stir, cover pot again and cook on high for 4 minutes more. Divide everything between plates and serve. Enjoy!

Beef Corn Chili

Preparation Time: 8-10 minutes

Cooking Time: 30 minutes

Servings: 8

Ingredients:

- 2 small onions, chopped (finely)
- ¼ cup canned corn
- 1 tablespoon oil
- 10 ounces lean ground beef
- 2 small chili peppers, diced

Directions:

1. Take your instant pot and place over dry kitchen surface; open its top lid and switch it on. Press. "SAUTE". In its Cooking pot, add and heat the oil. Add the onions, chili pepper, and beef; cook for 2-3 minutes until turn translucent and softened. Add the 3 cups water in the Cooking pot; combine to mix well.

2. Close its top lid and make sure that its valve it closed to avoid spilling. Press "MEAT/STEW". Adjust the timer to 20 minutes. Press will slowly build up; let the added ingredients to cook until the timer indicates zero. Press "CANCEL". Now press "NPR" for natural release pressure. Instant pot will gradually release pressure for about 8-10 minutes. Open the top lid; transfer the cooked recipe in serving plates. Serve the recipe warm.

Balsamic Beef Dish

Preparation Time: 5 minutes

Cooking Time: 55 minutes

Servings: 8

Ingredients:

- 3 pounds chuck roast
- 3 cloves garlic, thinly sliced
- 1 tablespoon oil
- 1 teaspoon flavored vinegar
- ½ teaspoon pepper
- ½ teaspoon rosemary
- 1 tablespoon butter
- ½ teaspoon thyme
- ¼ cup balsamic vinegar
- 1 cup beef broth

Directions:

1. Cut slits in the roast and stuff garlic slices all over. Take a bowl and add flavored vinegar, rosemary, pepper, thyme and rub the mixture over the roast. Set your pot to sauté mode and add oil, allow the oil to heat up. Add roast and brown both sides (5 minutes each side).

2. Take the roast out and keep it on the side. Add butter, broth, balsamic vinegar and deglaze the pot. Transfer the roast back and lock up the lid, cook on HIGH pressure for 40 minutes.

3. Perform a quick release. Remove the lid and serve!

Soy Sauce Beef Roast

Preparation Time: 8 minutes

Cooking Time: 35 minutes

Servings: 2-3

Ingredients:

- ½ teaspoon beef bouillon
- 1 ½ teaspoon rosemary
- ½ teaspoon minced garlic
- 2 pounds roast beef
- 1/3 cup soy sauce

Directions:

1. Mix the soy sauce, bouillon, rosemary, and garlic together in a mixing bowl. Place your instant pot over as dry kitchen platform. Open the top lid and plug it on. Add the roast, bowl mix and enough water to cover the roast; gently stir to mix well. Properly close the top lid; make sure that the safety valve is properly locked.

2. Press "MEAT/STEW" Cooking function; set pressure level to "HIGH" and set the Cooking time to 35 minutes. Allow the pressure to build to cook the ingredients. After Cooking time is over press "CANCEL" setting. Find and press "NPR" Cooking function. This setting is for the natural release of inside pressure, and it takes around 10 minutes to slowly release pressure.

3. Slowly open the lid, take out the cooked meat and shred it. Add the shredded meat back in the potting mix and stir to mix well. Take out the cooked recipe in serving containers. Serve warm.

Rosemary Beef Chuck Roast

Preparation Time: 5 minutes

Cooking Time: 45 minutes

Servings: 5-6

Ingredients:

- 3 pounds chuck beef roast
- 3 garlic cloves
- ¼ cup balsamic vinegar
- 1 sprig fresh rosemary
- 1 sprig fresh thyme
- 1 cup of water
- 1 tablespoon vegetable oil
- Salt and pepper to taste

Directions:

1. Cut slices in the beef roast and place the garlic cloves in them. Coat the roast with the herbs, black pepper, and salt. Preheat your instant pot using the sauté setting and add the oil. When warmed, add the beef roast and stir-

47

cook until browned on all sides. Add the remaining ingredients; stir gently.

2. Seal the lid and cook on high pressure for 40 minutes using the manual setting. Let the pressure release naturally, about 10 minutes. Uncover the instant pot; transfer the beef roast the serving plates, slice and serve.

Pork Chops and Tomato Sauce

Preparation Time: 10 minutes

Cooking Time: 20 minutes

Servings: 4

Ingredients:

- 4 pork chops, boneless
- 1 tablespoon soy sauce
- ¼ teaspoon sesame oil
- 1 and ½ cups tomato paste
- 1 yellow onion
- 8 mushrooms, sliced

Directions:

In a bowl, mix pork chops with soy sauce and sesame oil, toss and leave aside for 10 minutes. Set your instant pot on sauté mode, add pork chops and brown them for 5 minutes on each side. Add onion, stir and cook for 1-2 minutes more.

Add tomato paste and mushrooms, toss, cover and cook on high for 8-9 minutes. Divide everything between plates and serve. Enjoy!

Chicken with Caper Sauce

Preparation Time: 20 minutes

Cooking Time: 18 minutes

Servings: 5

Ingredients:

For Chicken:

- 2 eggs
- Salt and ground black pepper, as required
- 1 cup dry breadcrumbs
- 2 tablespoons olive oil
- 1½ pounds skinless, boneless chicken breast halves, pounded into ¾inch thickness and cut into pieces

For Capers Sauce:

- 3 tablespoons capers
- ½ cup dry white wine
- 3 tablespoons fresh lemon juice
- Salt and ground black pepper, as required
- 2 tablespoons fresh parsley, chopped

Directions:

1. For chicken: in a shallow dish, add the eggs, salt and black pepper and beat until well combined. In another shallow dish, place breadcrumbs. Dip the chicken pieces in egg mixture then coat with the breadcrumbs evenly. Shake off the excess breadcrumbs.

2. In a large skillet, heat the oil over medium heat and cook the chicken pieces for about 5-7 minutes per side or until desired doneness. With a slotted spoon, transfer the chicken pieces onto a paper towel lined plate. With a piece of the foil, cover the chicken pieces to keep them warm.

3. In the same skillet, add all the sauce ingredients except parsley and cook for about 2-3 minutes, stirring continuously. Stir in the parsley and remove from heat. Serve the chicken pieces with the topping of capers sauce.

Dinner

Garlic Chicken with Couscous

Preparation Time: 25 minutes

Cooking Time: 7 hours

Servings: 4

Ingredients:

- 1 whole chicken, cut into pieces
- 1 tablespoon extra-virgin olive oil
- 6 cloves garlic, halved
- 1 cup dry white wine
- 1 cup couscous
- ½ teaspoon salt
- ½ teaspoon pepper
- 1 medium onion, thinly sliced
- 2 teaspoons dried thyme
- 1/3 cup whole wheat flour

Directions:

1. Heat the olive oil in a heavy skillet. When skillet is hot, add the chicken to sear. Make sure the chicken pieces don't touch each other. Cook with the skin side down for about 3 minutes or until browned.

2. Spray your slow cooker with nonstick cooking spray or olive oil. Put the onion, garlic, and thyme into the slow cooker and sprinkle with salt and pepper. Add the chicken on top of the onions.

3. In a separate bowl, whisk the flour into the wine until there are no lumps, then pour over the chicken. Cook the chicken on low for 7 hours or until done. You can cook on high for 3 hours as well. Serve the chicken over the cooked couscous and spoon sauce over the top.

Chicken Karahi

Preparation Time: 5 minutes

Cooking Time: 5 hours

Servings: 4

Ingredients:

- 2 pounds chicken breasts or thighs, cut into bite-sized pieces
- ¼ cup olive oil
- 1 small can tomato paste
- 1 tablespoon butter
- 1 large onion, diced
- ½ cup plain Greek yogurt
- ½ cup water
- 2 tablespoons ginger in garlic paste
- 3 tablespoons fenugreek leaves
- 1 teaspoon ground coriander
- 1 medium tomato
- 1 teaspoon red chili
- 2 green chilies

- 1 teaspoon turmeric
- 1 tablespoon garam masala
- 1 teaspoon cumin powder
- 1 teaspoon sea salt
- ¼ teaspoon nutmeg

Directions:

1. Spray the slow cooker with nonstick cooking spray. In a small bowl, thoroughly mix together all of the spices. Add the chicken to the slow cooker followed by the rest of the ingredients, including the spice mixture. Stir until everything is well mixed with the spices.
2. Cook on low for 4–5 hours. Serve with naan or Italian bread.

Chicken Cacciatore with Orzo

Preparation Time: 20 minutes

Cooking Time: 4 hours

Servings: 6

Ingredients:

- 2 pounds skin-on chicken thighs
- 1 tablespoon olive oil
- 1 cup mushrooms, quartered
- 3 carrots, chopped
- 1 small jar Kalamata olives
- 2 (14-ounce) cans diced tomatoes
- 1 small can tomato paste
- 1 cup red wine
- 5 garlic cloves, peeled and crushed
- 1 cup orzo

Directions:

1. In a large skillet, heat the olive oil over medium-high heat. When the oil is heated, add the chicken, skin side down, and sear it. Make sure the pieces of chicken don't touch each other.

2. When the chicken is browned, add to the slow cooker along with all the ingredients except the orzo. Cook the chicken on low for 2 hours, then add the orzo and cook for an additional 2 hours. Serve with a crusty French bread.

Slow Cooked Daube Provencal

Preparation Time: 15 minutes

Cooking Time: 8 hours

Servings: 8

Ingredients:

- 1 tablespoon olive oil
- 10 garlic cloves, minced
- 2 pounds boneless chuck roast, trimmed and cut into 2-inch cubes
- 1½ teaspoons salt, divided
- ½ teaspoon freshly ground black pepper
- 1 cup dry red wine
- 2 cups carrots, chopped
- 1½ cups onion, chopped
- ½ cup beef broth
- 1 (14-ounce) can diced tomatoes
- 1 tablespoon tomato paste
- 1 teaspoon fresh rosemary, chopped
- 1 teaspoon fresh thyme, chopped

- ½ teaspoon orange zest, grated
- ½ teaspoon ground cinnamon
- ¼ teaspoon ground cloves
- 1 bay leaf

Directions:

1. Heat a skillet and then add the olive oil. Add the minced garlic and onions and cook until the onions are soft and the garlic begins to brown.

2. Add the cubed meat, salt, and pepper and cook until the meat has browned. Transfer the meat to the slow cooker. Add the beef broth to the skillet and let simmer for about 3 minutes to deglaze the pan, then pour into slow cooker over the meat.

3. Add the rest of the ingredients to the slow cooker and stir well to combine. Set your slow cooker to low and cook for 8 hours, or set to high and cook for 4 hours. Serve with a side of egg noodles, rice or some crusty Italian bread.

Osso Bucco

Preparation Time: 30 minutes

Cooking Time: 8 hours

Servings: 3

Ingredients:

- 4 beef shanks or veal shanks
- 1 teaspoon sea salt
- ½ teaspoon ground black pepper
- 3 tablespoons whole wheat flour
- 1–2 tablespoons olive oil
- 2 medium onions, diced
- 2 medium carrots, diced
- 2 celery stalks, diced
- 4 garlic cloves, minced
- 1 (14-ounce) can diced tomatoes
- 2 teaspoons dried thyme leaves
- ½ cup beef or vegetable stock

Directions:

1. Season the shanks with salt and pepper on both sides, then dip in the flour to coat. Heat a large skillet over high heat. Add the olive oil. When the oil is hot, add the shanks and brown evenly on both sides. When browned, transfer to the slow cooker.

2. Pour the stock into the skillet and let simmer for 3–5 minutes while stirring to deglaze the pan. Add the rest of the ingredients to the slow cooker and pour the stock from the skillet over the top.

3. Set the slow cooker to low and cook for 8 hours. Serve the Osso Bucco over quinoa, brown rice, or even cauliflower rice.

Slow Cooker Beef Bourguignon

Preparation Time: 5 minutes

Cooking Time: 8 hours

Servings: 8

Ingredients:

- 1 tablespoon extra-virgin olive oil
- 6 ounces bacon, roughly chopped
- 3 pounds beef brisket, trimmed of fat, cut into 2-inch cubes
- 1 large carrot, sliced
- 1 large white onion, diced
- 6 cloves garlic, minced and divided
- ½ teaspoon coarse salt
- ½ teaspoon freshly ground pepper
- 2 tablespoons whole wheat
- 12 small pearl onions
- 3 cups red wine (Merlot, Pinot Noir, or Chianti)
- 2 cups beef stock
- 2 tablespoons tomato paste

- 1 beef bouillon cube, crushed
- 1 teaspoon fresh thyme, finely chopped
- 2 tablespoons fresh parsley, finely chopped and divided
- 2 bay leaves
- 2 tablespoons butter or 1 tablespoon olive oil
- 1 pound fresh small white or brown mushrooms, quartered

Directions:

1. Heat a skillet over medium-high heat, then add the olive oil. When the oil has heated, cook the bacon until it is crisp, then place it in your slow cooker. Save the bacon fat in the skillet.

2. Dry the beef with a paper towel and cook it in the same skillet with the bacon fat until all sides have the same brown coloring. Transfer to the slow cooker.

3. Add the onions and carrots to the slow cooker and season with the salt and pepper. Stir to combine the ingredients and make sure everything is seasoned.

4. Pour the red wine into the skillet and simmer for 4–5 minutes to deglaze the pan, then whisk in the flour,

stirring until smooth. Continue cooking until the liquid reduces and thickens a bit.

5. When the liquid has thickened, pour it into the slow cooker and stir to coat everything with the wine mixture. Add the tomato paste, bouillon cube, thyme, parsley, 4 cloves of garlic, and bay leaf. Set your slow cooker to high and cook for 6 hours, or set to low and cook for 8 hours.

6. Just before you are ready to serve, melt the butter or heat the olive oil in a skillet over medium heat. When the oil is hot, add the remaining 2 cloves of garlic and cook for about 1 minute before adding the mushrooms. Cook the mushrooms until soft, then add to the slow cooker and mix to combine.

7. Serve with mashed potatoes, rice or noodles.

Balsamic Beef

Preparation Time: 5 minutes

Cooking Time: 8 hours

Servings: 10

Ingredients:

- 2 pounds boneless chuck roast
- 1 tablespoon olive oil
- Rub
- 1 teaspoon garlic powder
- ½ teaspoon onion powder
- 1 teaspoon sea salt
- ½ teaspoon freshly ground black pepper
- Sauce
- ½ cup balsamic vinegar
- 2 tablespoons honey
- 1 tablespoon honey mustard
- 1 cup beef broth
- 1 tablespoon tapioca, whole wheat flour, or cornstarch (to thicken sauce when it is done cooking if desired)

Directions:

1. Mix together all of the ingredients for the rub.

2. In a separate bowl, mix the balsamic vinegar, honey, and honey mustard, and beef broth. Coat the roast in olive oil, then rub in the spices from the rub mix. Place the roast in the slow cooker and then pour the sauce over the top. Set the slow cooker to low and cook for 8 hours.

3. If you want to thicken the sauce when the roast is done cooking transfer it from the slow cooker to a serving plate. Then pour the liquid into a saucepan and heat to boiling on the stovetop. Whisk in the flour until smooth and let simmer until the sauce thickens.

Veal Pot Roast

Preparation Time: 20 minutes

Cooking Time: 5 hours

Servings: 8

Ingredients:

- 2 tablespoons olive oil
- Salt and pepper
- 3-pound boneless veal roast, tied
- 4 medium carrots, peeled
- 2 parsnips, peeled and halved
- 2 white turnips, peeled and quartered
- 10 garlic cloves, peeled
- 2 sprigs fresh thyme
- 1 orange, scrubbed and zested
- 1 cup chicken or veal stock

Directions:

1. Heat a large skillet over medium-high heat. Rub veal roast all over with olive oil, then season with salt and pepper. When the skillet is hot, add the veal roast and

sear on all sides. This will take about 3 minutes on every side, but this process seals in the juices and makes the meat succulent.

2. When the roast is brown on all sides, transfer it to the slow cooker. Toss the carrots, parsnips, turnips, and garlic into the skillet. Stir and cook for about 5 minutes—not all the way through, just to get some of the brown bits from the veal and give them a bit of color.

3. Transfer the vegetables to the slow cooker, placing them all around the meat. Top the roast with the thyme and the zest from the orange. Cut the orange in half and squeeze the juice over the top of the meat. Add the chicken stock, then cook the roast on low for 5 hours.

Mediterranean Rice and Sausage

Preparation Time: 15 minutes

Cooking Time: 8 hours

Servings: 6

Ingredients:

- 1½ pounds Italian sausage, crumbled
- 1 medium onion, chopped
- 2 tablespoons steak sauce
- 2 cups long grain rice, uncooked
- 1 (14-ounce) can diced tomatoes with juice
- ½ cup water
- 1 medium green pepper, diced

Directions:

1. Spray your slow cooker with olive oil or nonstick cooking spray. Add the sausage, onion, and steak sauce to the slow cooker. Cook on low for 8 to 10 hours.

2. After 8 hours, add the rice, tomatoes, water and green pepper. Stir to combine thoroughly. Cook an additional 20 to 25 minutes or until the rice is cooked.

Spanish Meatballs

Preparation Time: 20 minutes

Cooking Time: 5 hours

Servings: 6

Ingredients:

- 1-pound ground turkey
- 1-pound ground pork
- 2 eggs
- 1 (20-ounce) can diced tomatoes
- ¾ cup sweet onion, minced, divided
- ¼ cup plus 1 tablespoon breadcrumbs
- 3 tablespoons fresh parsley, chopped
- 1½ teaspoons cumin
- 1½ teaspoons paprika (sweet or hot)

Directions:

1. Spray the slow cooker with olive oil.
2. In a mixing bowl, combine the ground meat, eggs, about half of the onions, the breadcrumbs, and the spices.

3. Wash your hands and mix together until everything is well combined. Do not over-mix, though, as this makes for tough meatballs. Shape into meatballs. How big you make them will obviously determine how many total meatballs you get.

4. In a skillet, heat 2 tablespoons of olive oil over medium heat. When the skillet and oil are hot, add the meatballs and brown on all sides. Make sure the balls aren't touching each other so they brown evenly. When they are done, transfer them to the slow cooker.

5. Add the rest of the onions and the tomatoes to the skillet and allow them to cook for a few minutes, scraping the brown bits from the meatballs up to add flavor. Pour the tomatoes over the meatballs in the slow cooker and cook on low for 5 hours.

Snacks

Zucchini Feta Roulades

Preparation Time: 10 minutes

Cooking Time: 10 minutes

Servings: 6

Ingredients:

½ cup feta

1 garlic clove, minced

2 tablespoons fresh basil, minced

1 tablespoon capers, minced

1/8 teaspoon salt

1/8 teaspoon red pepper flakes

1 tablespoon lemon juice

2 medium zucchinis

12 toothpicks

Directions:

1. Preheat the air fryer to 360°F. (If using a grill attachment, make sure it is inside the air fryer during preheating.) In a small bowl, combine the feta, garlic, basil, capers, salt, red pepper flakes, and lemon juice.

2. Slice the zucchini into 1/8-inch strips lengthwise. (Each zucchini should yield around 6 strips.)

3. Spread 1 tablespoon of the cheese filling onto each slice of zucchini, then roll it up and secure it with a toothpick through the middle.

4. Place the zucchini roulades into the air fryer basket in a single layer, making sure that they don't touch each other.

5. Bake or grill in the air fryer for 10 minutes.

6. Remove the zucchini roulades from the air fryer and gently remove the toothpicks before serving.

Garlic-Roasted Tomatoes and Olives

Preparation Time: 5 minutes

Cooking Time: 20 minutes

Servings: 6

Ingredients:

- 2 cups cherry tomatoes
- 4 garlic cloves, roughly chopped
- ½ red onion, roughly chopped
- 1 cup black olives
- 1 cup green olives
- 1 tablespoon fresh basil, minced
- 1 tablespoon fresh oregano, minced
- 2 tablespoons olive oil
- ¼ to ½ teaspoon salt

Directions:

1. Preheat the air fryer to 380°F. In a large bowl, combine all of the ingredients and toss together so that the

tomatoes and olives are coated well with the olive oil and herbs.

2. Pour the mixture into the air fryer basket, and roast for 10 minutes. Stir the mixture well, then continue roasting for an additional 10 minutes. Remove from the air fryer, transfer to a serving bowl, and enjoy.

Hummus with Ground Lamb

Preparation Time: 10 minutes

Cooking Time: 15 minutes

Servings: 8

Ingredients:

- 10 ounces hummus
- 12 ounces lamb meat, ground
- ½ cup pomegranate seeds
- ¼ cup parsley, chopped
- 1 tablespoon olive oil
- Pita chips for serving

Directions:

1. Preheat pan over medium-high heat, cook the meat, and brown for 15 minutes stirring often.
2. Spread the hummus on a platter, spread the ground lamb all over, also spread the pomegranate seeds and the parsley and serve with pita chips as a snack.

Eggplant Dip

Preparation Time: 10 minutes

Cooking Time: 40 minutes

Servings: 4

Ingredients:

- 1 eggplant, poked with a fork
- 2 tablespoons tahini paste
- 2 tablespoons lemon juice
- 2 garlic cloves, minced
- 1 tablespoon olive oil
- Salt and black pepper to the taste
- 1 tablespoon parsley, chopped

Directions:

Put the eggplant in a roasting pan, bake at 400 degrees F for 40 minutes, cool down, peel and transfer to your food processor. Add the rest of the ingredients except the parsley, pulse well, divide into small bowls and serve as an appetizer with the parsley sprinkled on top.

Artichoke and Olive Pita Flatbread

Preparation Time: 5 minutes

Cooking Time: 10 minutes

Servings: 4

Ingredients:

- 2 whole wheat pitas
- 2 tablespoons olive oil, divided
- 2 garlic cloves, minced
- ¼ teaspoon salt
- ½ cup canned artichoke hearts, sliced
- ¼ cup Kalamata olives
- ¼ cup shredded Parmesan
- ¼ cup crumbled feta
- Chopped fresh parsley, for garnish (optional)

Directions:

1. Preheat the air fryer to 380°F. Brush each pita with 1 tablespoon olive oil, then sprinkle the minced garlic and salt over the top.

2. Distribute the artichoke hearts, olives, and cheeses evenly between the two pitas, and place both into the air fryer to bake for 10 minutes. Remove the pitas and cut them into 4 pieces each before serving. Sprinkle parsley over the top, if desired.

Goat Cheese and Garlic Crostini

Preparation Time: 3 minutes

Cooking Time: 5 minutes

Servings: 4

Ingredients:

- 1 whole wheat baguette
- ¼ cup olive oil
- 2 garlic cloves, minced
- 4 ounces goat cheese
- 2 tablespoons fresh basil, minced

Directions:

1. Preheat the air fryer to 380°F. Cut the baguette into ½-inch-thick slices. In a small bowl, mix together the olive oil and garlic, then brush it over one side of each slice of bread.
2. Place the olive-oil-coated bread in a single layer in the air fryer basket and bake for 5 minutes. Meanwhile, in a small bowl, mix together the goat cheese and basil.

3. Remove the toast from the air fryer, then spread a thin layer of the goat cheese mixture over the top of each piece and serve.

Rosemary-Roasted Red Potatoes

Preparation Time: 5 minutes

Cooking Time: 20 minutes

Servings: 6

Ingredients:

- 1-pound red potatoes, quartered
- ¼ cup olive oil
- ½ teaspoon kosher salt
- ¼ teaspoon black pepper
- 1 garlic clove, minced
- 4 rosemary sprigs

Directions:

1. Preheat the air fryer to 360°F.
2. In a large bowl, toss the potatoes with the olive oil, salt, pepper, and garlic until well coated.
3. Pour the potatoes into the air fryer basket and top with the sprigs of rosemary.

4. Roast for 10 minutes, then stir or toss the potatoes and roast for 10 minutes more.
5. Remove the rosemary sprigs and serve the potatoes.
6. Season with additional salt and pepper, if needed.

Baked Spanakopita Dip

Preparation Time: 10 minutes

Cooking Time: 15 minutes

Servings: 2

Ingredients:

- Olive oil cooking spray
- 3 tablespoons olive oil, divided
- 2 tablespoons minced white onion
- 2 garlic cloves, minced
- 4 cups fresh spinach
- 4 ounces cream cheese, softened
- 4 ounces feta cheese, divided
- Zest of 1 lemon
- ¼ teaspoon ground nutmeg
- 1 teaspoon dried dill
- ½ teaspoon salt
- Pita chips, carrot sticks, or sliced bread for serving (optional)

Directions:

Preheat the air fryer to 360°F. Coat the inside of a 6-inch ramekin or baking dish with olive oil cooking spray.

1. In a large skillet over medium heat, heat 1 tablespoon of the olive oil. Add the onion, then cook for 1 minute. Add in the garlic and cook, stirring for 1 minute more.

2. Reduce the heat to low and mix in the spinach and water. Let this cook for 2 to 3 minutes, or until the spinach has wilted. Remove the skillet from the heat. In a medium bowl, combine the cream cheese, 2 ounces of the feta, and the remaining 2 tablespoons of olive oil, along with the lemon zest, nutmeg, dill, and salt. Mix until just combined.

3. Add the vegetables to the cheese base and stir until combined. Pour the dip mixture into the prepared ramekin and top with the remaining 2 ounces of feta cheese.

4. Place the dip into the air fryer basket and cook for 10 minutes, or until heated through and bubbling. Serve with pita chips, carrot sticks, or sliced bread.

Roasted Pearl Onion Dip

Preparation Time: 5 minutes

Cooking Time: 12 minutes plus 1 hour to chill

Servings: 4

Ingredients:

- 2 cups peeled pearl onions
- 3 garlic cloves
- 3 tablespoons olive oil, divided
- ½ teaspoon salt
- 1 cup nonfat plain Greek yogurt
- 1 tablespoon lemon juice
- ¼ teaspoon black pepper
- 1/8 teaspoon red pepper flakes
- Pita chips, vegetables, or toasted bread for serving (optional)

Directions:

1. Preheat the air fryer to 360°F. In a large bowl, combine the pearl onions and garlic with 2 tablespoons of the olive oil until the onions are well coated.

2. Pour the garlic-and-onion mixture into the air fryer basket and roast for 12 minutes. Transfer the garlic and onions to a food processor. Pulse the vegetables several times, until the onions are minced but still have some chunks.

3. In a large bowl, combine the garlic and onions and the remaining 1 tablespoon of olive oil, along with the salt, yogurt, lemon juice, black pepper, and red pepper flakes. Cover and chill for 1 hour before serving with pita chips, vegetables, or toasted bread.

Red Pepper Tapenade

Preparation Time: 5 minutes

Cooking Time: 5 minutes

Servings: 4

Ingredients:

- 1 large red bell pepper
- 2 tablespoons plus 1 teaspoon olive oil, divided
- ½ cup Kalamata olives, pitted and roughly chopped
- 1 garlic clove, minced
- ½ teaspoon dried oregano
- 1 tablespoon lemon juice

Directions:

1. Preheat the air fryer to 380°F. Brush the outside of a whole red pepper with 1 teaspoon olive oil and place it inside the air fryer basket. Roast for 5 minutes.

2. Meanwhile, in a medium bowl combine the remaining 2 tablespoons of olive oil with the olives, garlic, oregano, and lemon juice.

3. Remove the red pepper from the air fryer, then gently slice off the stem and remove the seeds. Roughly chop the roasted pepper into small pieces.

4. Add the red pepper to the olive mixture and stir all together until combined. Serve with pita chips, crackers, or crusty bread.

Greek Potato Skins with Olives and Feta

Preparation Time: 5 minutes

Cooking Time: 45 minutes

Servings: 4

Ingredients:

- 2 russet potatoes
- 3 tablespoons olive oil, divided, plus more for drizzling (optional)
- 1 teaspoon kosher salt, divided
- ¼ teaspoon black pepper
- 2 tablespoons fresh cilantro, chopped, plus more for serving
- ¼ cup Kalamata olives, diced
- ¼ cup crumbled feta
- Chopped fresh parsley, for garnish (optional)

Directions:

1. Preheat the air fryer to 380°F. Using a fork, poke 2 to 3 holes in the potatoes, then coat each with about ½ tablespoon olive oil and ½ teaspoon salt.

2. Place the potatoes into the air fryer basket and bake for 30 minutes. Remove the potatoes from the air fryer, and slice in half. Using a spoon, scoop out the flesh of the potatoes, leaving a ½-inch layer of potato inside the skins, and set the skins aside.

3. In a medium bowl, combine the scooped potato middles with the remaining 2 tablespoons of olive oil, ½ teaspoon of salt, black pepper, and cilantro. Mix until well combined. Divide the potato filling into the now-empty potato skins, spreading it evenly over them. Top each potato with a tablespoon each of the olives and feta.

4. Place the loaded potato skins back into the air fryer and bake for 15 minutes. Serve with additional chopped cilantro or parsley and a drizzle of olive oil, if desired.

Desserts

Cinnamon-Stewed Dried Plums with Greek Yogurt

Preparation Time: 10 minutes

Cooking Time: 15 minutes

Servings: 6

Ingredients:

- 3 cups dried plums
- 2 cups water
- 2 tablespoons sugar
- 2 cinnamon sticks
- 3 cups low-fat plain Greek yogurt

Directions:

1. Add dried plums, water, sugar, and cinnamon to the Instant Pot®. Close lid, set steam release to Sealing, press the Manual button, and set time to 3 minutes.

2. When the timer beeps, quick-release the pressure until the float valve drops. Press the Cancel button and open lid. Remove and discard cinnamon sticks. Serve warm over Greek yogurt.

Vanilla-Poached Apricots

Preparation Time: 10 minutes

Cooking Time: 20 minutes

Servings: 6

Ingredients:

- 1¼ cups water
- ¼ cup Marsala wine
- ¼ cup sugar
- 1 teaspoon vanilla bean paste
- 8 medium apricots, sliced in half and pitted

Directions:

1. Place all ingredients in the Instant Pot®. Stir to combine. Close lid, set steam release to Sealing, press the Manual button, and set time to 1 minute.
2. When the timer beeps, quick-release the pressure until the float valve drops. Press the Cancel button and open lid. Let stand for 10 minutes. Carefully remove apricots from poaching liquid with a slotted spoon. Serve warm or at room temperature.

Creamy Spiced Almond Milk

Preparation Time: 10 minutes

Cooking Time: 15 minutes

Servings: 6

Ingredients:

- 1 cup raw almonds
- 5 cups filtered water, divided
- 1 teaspoon vanilla bean paste
- ½ teaspoon pumpkin pie spice

Directions:

1. Add almonds and 1 cup water to the Instant Pot®. Close lid, set steam release to Sealing, press the Manual button, and set time to 1 minute.
2. When the timer beeps, quick-release the pressure until the float valve drops. Press the Cancel button and open lid. Strain almonds and rinse under cool water. Transfer to a high-powered blender with remaining 4 cups water. Purée for 2 minutes on high speed.

3. Pour mixture into a nut milk bag set over a large bowl. Squeeze bag to extract all liquid. Stir in vanilla and pumpkin pie spice. Transfer to a Mason jar or sealed jug and refrigerate for 8 hours. Stir or shake gently before serving.

Poached Pears with Greek Yogurt and Pistachio

Preparation Time: 10 minutes

Cooking Time: 15 minutes

Servings: 8

Ingredients:

- 2 cups water
- 1¾ cups apple cider
- ¼ cup lemon juice
- 1 cinnamon stick
- 1 teaspoon vanilla bean paste
- 4 large Bartlett pears, peeled
- 1 cup low-fat plain Greek yogurt
- ½ cup unsalted roasted pistachio meats

Directions:

1. Add water, apple cider, lemon juice, cinnamon, vanilla, and pears to the Instant Pot®. Close lid, set steam release to Sealing, press the Manual button, and set time to 3 minutes.

2. When the timer beeps, quick-release the pressure until the float valve drops. Press the Cancel button and open lid. With a slotted spoon remove pears to a plate and allow to cool to room temperature.

3. To serve, carefully slice pears in half with a sharp paring knife and scoop out core with a melon baller.

4. Lay pear halves on dessert plates or in shallow bowls. Top with yogurt and garnish with pistachios.

5. Serve immediately.

Peaches Poached in Rose Water

Preparation Time: 10 minutes

Cooking Time: 20 minutes

Servings: 6

Ingredients:

- 1 cup water
- 1 cup rose water
- ¼ cup wildflower honey
- 8 green cardamom pods, lightly crushed
- 1 teaspoon vanilla bean paste
- 6 large yellow peaches, pitted and quartered
- ½ cup chopped unsalted roasted pistachio meats

Directions:

1. Add water, rose water, honey, cardamom, and vanilla to the Instant Pot®. Whisk well, then add peaches. Close lid, set steam release to Sealing, press the Manual button, and set time to 1 minute.

2. When the timer beeps, quick-release the pressure until the float valve drops. Press the Cancel button and open lid. Allow peaches to stand for 10 minutes. Carefully remove peaches from poaching liquid with a slotted spoon.

3. Slip skins from peach slices. Arrange slices on a plate and garnish with pistachios.

4. Serve warm or at room temperature.

Brown Betty Apple Dessert

Preparation Time: 10 minutes

Cooking Time: 10 minutes

Servings: 8

Ingredients:

- 2 cups dried bread crumbs
- ½ cup sugar
- 1 teaspoon ground cinnamon
- 3 tablespoons lemon juice
- 1 tablespoon grated lemon zest
- 1 cup olive oil, divided
- 8 medium apples, peeled, cored, and diced
- 2 cups water

Directions:

1. Combine crumbs, sugar, cinnamon, lemon juice, lemon zest, and ½ cup oil in a medium mixing bowl. Set aside.
2. In a greased oven-safe dish that will fit in your cooker loosely, add a thin layer of crumbs, then one diced apple.

Continue filling the container with alternating layers of crumbs and apples until all ingredients are finished. Pour remaining ½ cup oil on top.

3. Add water to the Instant Pot® and place rack inside. Make a foil sling by folding a long piece of foil in half lengthwise and lower the uncovered container into the pot using the sling.

4. Close lid, set steam release to Sealing, press the Manual button, and set time to 10 minutes. When the timer beeps, let pressure release naturally, about 20 minutes. Press the Cancel button and open lid. Using the sling, remove the baking dish from the pot and let stand for 5 minutes before serving.

Blueberry Oat Crumble

Preparation Time: 10 minutes

Cooking Time: 10 minutes

Servings: 8

Ingredients:

- 1 cup water
- 4 cups blueberries
- 2 tablespoons packed light brown sugar
- 2 tablespoons cornstarch
- 1/8 teaspoon ground nutmeg
- 1/3 cup rolled oats
- ¼ cup granulated sugar
- ¼ cup all-purpose flour
- ¼ teaspoon ground cinnamon
- ¼ cup unsalted butter, melted and cooled

Directions:

1. Spray a baking dish that fits inside the Instant Pot® with nonstick cooking spray. Add water to the pot and add

rack. Fold a long piece of aluminum foil in half lengthwise. Lay foil over rack to form a sling.

2. In a medium bowl, combine blueberries, brown sugar, cornstarch, and nutmeg. Transfer mixture to prepared dish.

3. In a separate medium bowl, add oats, sugar, flour, and cinnamon. Mix well. Add butter and combine until mixture is crumbly. Sprinkle crumbles over blueberries, cover dish with aluminum foil, and crimp edges tightly.

4. Add baking dish to rack in pot so it rests on the sling and close lid. Set steam release to Sealing, press the Manual button, and set time to 10 minutes.

5. When the timer beeps, let pressure release naturally for 10 minutes, then quick-release the remaining pressure until the float valve drops. Press the Cancel button and open lid. Carefully remove dish with sling and remove foil cover.

6. Heat broiler on high. Broil crumble until topping is golden brown, about 5 minutes. Serve warm or at room temperature.

Date and Walnut Cookies

Preparation Time: 10 minutes

Cooking Time: 2 minutes

Servings: 30

Ingredients:

- 2 cups flour
- 1/4 cup sour cream
- 1/2 cup butter, softened
- 1 1/2 cups brown sugar
- 1/2 cup white sugar
- 1 egg
- 1 cup dates, pitted and chopped
- 1/3 cup water
- 1/4 cup walnuts, finely chopped
- 1/2 tsp salt
- 1/2 tsp baking soda
- A pinch of cinnamon

Directions:

1. Cook the dates together with the white sugar and water over medium-high heat, stirring constantly, until mixture is thick like jam. Add in the nuts, stir and remove from heat. Leave to cool.

2. In a medium bowl, beat the butter and brown sugar. Stir in the egg and the sour cream. Sift the flour together with salt, baking soda and cinnamon and stir it into the butter mixture. Drop a teaspoon of dough onto a cookie sheet, place 1/4 teaspoon of the filling on top of it and top with an additional 1/2 teaspoon of dough. Repeat with the rest of the dough. Bake cookies for about 10 minutes in a preheated to 340 F oven, or until golden.

Moroccan Stuffed Dates

Preparation Time: 15 minutes

Cooking Time: 0 minute

Servings: 30

Ingredients:

- 1 lb. dates
- 1 cup blanched almonds
- 1/4 cup sugar
- 1 1/2 tbsp. orange flower water
- 1 tbsp. butter, melted
- 1/4 teaspoon cinnamon

Directions:

1. Process the almonds, sugar and cinnamon in a food processor.
2. Add the butter and orange flower water and process until a smooth paste is formed.
3. Roll small pieces of almond paste the same length as a date.

4. Take one date, make a vertical cut and discard the pit.

5. Insert a piece of the almond paste and press the sides of the date firmly around.

6. Repeat with all the remaining dates and almond paste.

Fig Cookies

Preparation Time: 10 minutes

Cooking Time: 15 minutes

Servings: 24

Ingredients:

- 1 cup flour
- 1 egg
- 1/2 cup sugar
- 1/2 cup figs, chopped
- 1/2 cup butter
- 1/4 cup water
- 1/2 tsp vanilla extract
- 1 tsp baking powder
- A pinch of salt

Directions:

1. Cook figs with water, stirring, for 4-5 minutes, or until thickened. Set aside to cool. Beat butter with sugar until light and fluffy. Add in the egg and vanilla and beat to blend well. In another bowl, sift together flour, baking powder and salt. Blend this into the egg mixture. Stir in the cooled figs.

2. Drop teaspoonful of dough on a greased baking tray. Bake in a preheated to 375 F oven, for about 10 minutes, or until lightly browned. Remove cookies and cool on wire racks.

Conclusion

Overall, this book is a great resource for anyone who wants to learn more about the Mediterranean diet and how to cook healthy and delicious food. The Ultimate Mediterranean Cookbook is an awesome cookbook that will give you a broad variety of recipes from the Mediterranean region. The Mediterranean Diet is a diet that's been around for thousands of years and is full of healthy, plant-based foods. The main components of the diet are fruits, vegetables, whole grains, legumes and nuts.

The Ultimate Mediterranean Cookbook is the ultimate resource for anyone who loves to cook with the flavors of the Mediterranean, and it's a must-have for anybody who loves to cook!

The Ultimate Mediterranean Cookbook is a must-have for anyone who is looking to eat healthy and eat well. Eating healthy, exercising regularly, and drinking lots of water are the key to a long and healthy life.

I hope you enjoyed reading this Ultimate Mediterranean Cookbook review. I'm always looking for great new products and I'm sure there's another great product that could be added to the list. Mediterranean diets are based on the principles of eating whole foods, like fresh fruits and vegetables, lean meats, nuts, olive oil and fish. These types of diets have been shown to have many health benefits.

I hope you enjoyed this ultimate guide to the Mediterranean diet. It's a diet that's easy to follow and has been proven to improve health, reduce stress levels and make you look and feel amazing. Here are a few highlights from the book:

- The Mediterranean diet is a nutritional approach used to prevent, diagnose, and treat many diseases in the human body. With the rise in popularity of the Mediterranean diet, it's important to remember that this isn't about limiting yourself to one part of the world.

I want to take a moment to thank you for purchasing this book. I first got the idea for this book while I was studying at culinary school. This book contains over 300 recipes for Mediterranean dishes. Recipes include: meat, fish, poultry, vegetables and soups. I think that the Mediterranean diet is one of the healthiest and balanced diets you can follow. It's based on fresh vegetables, fruit, nuts, legumes and fish which are all healthy foods.

The Ultimate Mediterranean Cookbook is a great book that can be used as a reference guide when it comes to cooking for the Mediterranean diet. This essential cookbook is now in its sixth edition and has changed the way so many people cook. The Mediterranean diet not only promotes healthy eating and weight loss, but is also linked to better cognitive function and heart health. The Mediterranean diet is rich in fruits, vegetables, whole grains, legumes, nuts and seeds.

Notes:

CPSIA information can be obtained
at www.ICGtesting.com
Printed in the USA
LVHW081204110521
687091LV00004B/1045